THE SONGWRITER'S GUIDE TO MELODIES

This book deals with melodies constructed from various scale materials in much the same way as words, clauses, sentences, and paragraphs are created from the alphabet.

FOREWORD

Music consists of three elements – melody, harmony, and rhythm. This book deals with the creation of melodies derived from various materials. If put into practice, it will give you an endless wealth of concepts. You should never run out of new and interesting ideas.

It starts off very simply and then builds so that you can grow musically. No matter what your level, you'll find new ideas developing as you learn each section. The approach will be the same as learning a new language. You'll start by writing short, direct, clear ideas called "phrases," which are sections of the melody, similar to a clause or sentence in language. You'll then join and expand these phrases into complete songs.

The techniques and ideas described in this book are universal to all styles of music – popular, jazz, rock, country, classical, etc. No matter what your preference, this is the book that will finally "show you how."

CONTENTS

BOOKS BY JOE LILORE

WARNER BROS. PUBLICATIONS INC.

BASS SUPERSTAR SERIES:

Dokken	IFO379
Genesis	IFO219
Heart	IFO334
Led Zeppelin	IFO200
Motley Crue	IFO294
Rolling Stones	IFO218
R*U*S*H	IFO198
Scorpions	IFO217
Whitesnake	IFO361
Yes	IFO335

MODERN BASSIST SERIES:

Chord Dictionary for the Modern Bassist	IFO162
Classical Themes for the Modern Bassist	IFO316
Improvising Jazz Bass Lines and Solos	IFO208
Learning the Blues for the Modern Bassist	IFO175
Rock Bass Lines For the Modern Bassist	IFO296
Solos For the Modern Bassist	IFO324
The Modern Bassist - A Complete Method	IFO123

LEARNIN' THE BLUES SERIES:

Learnin' the Blues for Alto Sax	IFO185
Learnin' the Blues for Flute	IFO183
Learnin' the Blues for Guitar	GFO303
Learnin' the Blues for Piano	PFO337
Learnin' the Blues for Tenor Sax	IFO184
Learnin' the Blues for Trombone	IFO186
Learnin' the Blues for Trumpet	IFO182

LIONHEAD PUBLISHING

Guitar Chords for the 21st Century
The Songwriter's Guide to Melodies
The Songwriter's Guide to Chords and Progressions
59 Days to the Guitar

CHAPTER I

MUSICAL PHRASE

A **musical phrase** can be **compared to a clause or sentence in a paragraph.** The term **"phrase"** is **not a precise measurement,** but only a **general guideline** because of the **infinite variations** in **melodic construction.** When you write, **you combine related sentences, clauses, and phrases** to **convey a thought** or tell a story. In **music,** it is **exactly the same. You have to convey to the listener a logical and complete musical statement through the combination of these phrases.**

TWO-MEASURE MUSICAL PHRASES

The following examples are **musical phrases, two measures long, based on the Major Scale*.** All **movement** will be **diatonic** (stepwise in motion - no interval jumps) **for now.** When you **create your own phrases,** try and _"say"_ something to the listener **that makes sense through** your **choice of notes, movements, and direction.**

EXAMPLES: A.B.C. are based on the **C Major Scale.**

EX. A: This example **ends on the main note** (tonic) **of the Major Scale** being used, ending the phrase in the same manner a **period ends a sentence.**

EX. B: This example **ends on a scale tone other than the tonic,** giving the impression of a pause - **similar to a comma** in a sentence.

EX. C: You may **begin a phrase on the tonic,** or **any scale tone** you wish.

*Major Scales and Their Construction - Page 57.

6

The following examples of *two-bar phrases* begin and end with various scale tones.

EX. A - C MAJOR

TONIC

EX. B - D MAJOR

3 RD   TONIC

EX. C - F MAJOR

5 TH   6 TH

EX. D - G MAJOR

TONIC   TONIC

EX. E - Eb MAJOR

5 TH   2ND

EX. F - A MAJOR

5 TH   TONIC

EX. G - Bb MAJOR

3rd   2nd

EX. H - E MAJOR

TONIC   *   3rd

Now that you've studied the examples given, **compose your own two-bar phrases. Begin and end** your phrases **on various notes** of the **major scales,** moving in **stepwise motion only.** Pay **careful attention** to the *effect* created when you **begin or end** a phrase on the **tonic** or another scale tone. **Use as many rhythmic variation as possible.** Be sure you're able to **play and/or sing** them **yourself.** Keep in mind that **most great melodies are simple to understand** and **remember.**

*Pick-Up Notes (Anacrusis)

FOUR MEASURE PHRASES

The **following examples** are **four measures in length.** You **can use two short phrases** (Ex. A) **or one long Phrase** (Ex. B)*

EX. A.

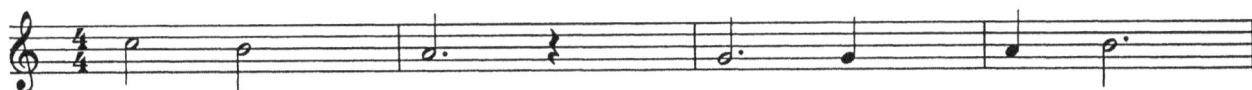

In "**Example A**", take notice that **the first phrase does not end on the tonic.** Keep this in mind **when combining and relating two short phrases.** This is **done so the listener will not feel it is the end of the thought**, but only a pause. However, **the end of the fourth measure** can end **either on the tonic** or **another scale tone.** Think of the **first phrase as a question** and the **second phrase as the answer.**

EX. B

TONIC   TONIC - END

In "**Example B**", there is **no pause halfway through.** It is **one continuous phrase,** leading to **a definite end or to a pause, depending on** your **choice of notes.**

You can **compare this to the writing** of **one long or two short thoughts in literature. Varying phrase lengths decrease monotony and increase musicality.**

The following examples are **four-bar phrases** using **various techniques. Play and study** each one **carefully.**

1.   Based on **C Scale. Two two-bar phrases.** The **1st phrase** pauses **on the 5th note of the scale.** The **2nd phrase,** completely different, **ends on the tonic.**

EX. 1

5 TH - PAUSE   TONIC

*In some books on composition, especially classical, the word "phrase" refers to 4-bar groupings only.

8

2. <u>Based on **G Scale**</u>. One four-bar phrase. Ends on tonic.

EX. 2

TONIC

3. <u>Based on **F Scale**</u>. Two two-bar phrases. The **2nd phrase** is a **repetition of the 1st** with the **last note changed** to end the thought. **Repetition** is **very essential** in creating music which is easily recognizable.

EX. 3

3rd   TONIC

4. <u>Based on **D Scale**</u>. Two two-bar phrases. The **2nd phrase** is a **repetition of the 1st with slight variations** to add interest.

EX. 4

PAUSE   PAUSE

5. <u>Based on **B♭ Scale**</u>. Two two-bar phrases. The **2nd phrase** is a **sequence based on the 1st phrase**. A **sequence** is an **imitation** of a phrase's **note pattern,** only **starting on a different note.**

EX. 5

PAUSE   PAUSE

6. <u>Based on **A Scale**</u>. Two two-bar phrases. The **2nd phrase** is a **sequence** of the **1st phrase with slight variations.**

EX. 6

7. Based on E♭ Scale. One four-bar phrase. The **2nd half** of the **phrase** is a **repetition** of the **1st.**

EX. 7

8. Based on **E Scale**. One four-bar phrase. The **2nd half** of the **phrase** is a **repetition** of the **first half with variation.**

EX. 8

9. Based on A♭ Scale. One four-bar phrase. The **2nd half** of the **phrase** is a **sequence** of the **first.**

EX. 9

10. Based on **B Scale**. One four-bar phrase. The **2nd half** of the **phrase** is a **sequence with variation.**

EX.10

The **opening four measures** of the world-famous **"Ode to Joy"** illustrate a **four bar phrase** moving in **diatonic step motion.**

ODE TO JOY

BEETHOVEN

STUDENT EXERCISES

Compose four-measure phrases (stepwise motion only), **using** the following **guidelines**:

	SCALE	1st NOTE	LAST NOTE	PHRASES
1.	C Scale	Tonic	Tonic	One Long
2.	F Scale	2nd	5th	Two Short*
3.	B♭ Scale	3rd	4th	One Long
4.	E♭ Scale	4th	3rd	Two Short
5.	A♭ Scale	5th	2nd	One Long
6.	G Scale	6th	6th	Two Short
7.	D Scale	7th	Tonic	One Long
8.	A Scale	Tonic	7th	Two Short

*Remember to use any scale tone **except** the tonic when pausing in the 2nd measure.

CHAPTER II

INTERVALS

We'll now **compose four measure phrases**, each one **stressing a different interval***. This is done so you'll **become accustomed to the sound of each interval** and its **particular role** in **creating a melody**. It's **very important that each melody makes sense** and **says something to the listener**. To accomplish this, I **strongly** **recommend** that you **not only play** - but **SING - everything you compose**. **Certain intervals** are **generally easier to sing** and, therefore, **fit into** the **melodic flow very easily**.

Constant experimenting will give you a **catalog of sounds to chose from** so you'll never be at a loss for **new ideas**. The **examples and exercises** on the following pages **emphasize** some of the most **commonly used intervals** in contemporary music.

NOTE: **Melody** is a **mixture** of **diatonic steps** and **various intervals** *woven* **together**. From this point on **you're not bound to move only in stepwise motion**.

*INTERVALS - the distance between two notes. See Pg. 60 for a complete explanation.

MAJOR 2nd - (M2)

The **interval of the major 2nd** will be found **between** the **following notes** of the **major scale**:

Example on "G"

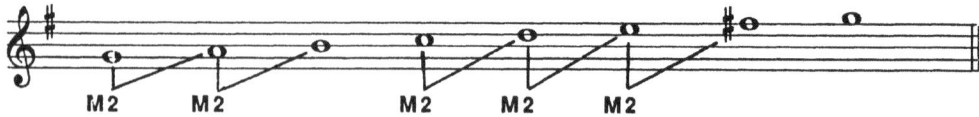

Compose a **four measure phrase, emphasizing** the **major 2nd**.

EXAMPLE:

MINOR 2nd - (m2)

The **interval of the minor 2nd** occurs **between** the **following notes** of the **major scale**:

Example on "F"

Compose a **four measure phrase, emphasizing** the **minor 2nd**.

EXAMPLE:

MAJOR 3rd - (M3)

The **interval of the Major 3rd** occurs **between** the **following notes** of the **major scale:**

Example on "B♭"

M3   M3 M3

Compose a **four measure** phrase, **emphasizing** the **major 3rd.**

EXAMPLE:

MINOR 3rd - (m3)

The **interval of the minor 3rd** occurs **between** the **following notes** of the **major scale:**

Example on "D"

m3   m3   m3

Compose a **four measure** phrase, **emphasizing** the **minor 3rd.**

EXAMPLE:

PERFECT 4th - (P4)

The **interval** of the **Perfect 4th** occurs **between** the **following notes** of the **major scale**:

Example on "E♭"

Compose a four measure phrase, emphasizing the Perfect 4th.

EXAMPLE:

PERFECT 5th - (P5)

The **interval** of the **Perfect 5th** occurs **between** the **following notes** of the **major scale**:

Example on "A♭"

Compose a four measure phrase, emphasizing the Perfect 5th.

EXAMPLE:

MAJOR 6th - (M6)

The **interval** of the **Major 6th** occurs **between** the **following notes** of the **major scale**:

Example on "D♭"

Compose a four measure phrase, emphasizing the Major 6th.

EXAMPLE:

16

MINOR 6th - (m6)

The **interval** of the **minor 6th** occurs **between** the **following notes** of the **major scale:**

Example on "B"

m6

Compose a **four measure phrase, emphasizing** the **minor 6th.**

EXAMPLE:

MAJOR 7th - (M7)

The **interval** of the **Major 7th** occurs **between** the **following notes** of the **major scale:**

Example on "E"

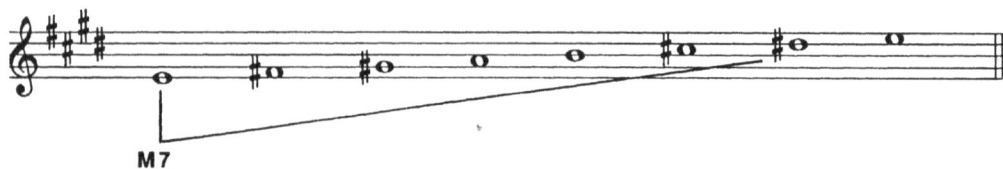

M7

Compose a **four measure phrase, emphasizing** the **Major 7th.**

EXAMPLE:

MINOR   7th - (m7)

The **interval** of the **minor 7th** occurs **between** the **following notes** of the **major scale:**

Example on "A"

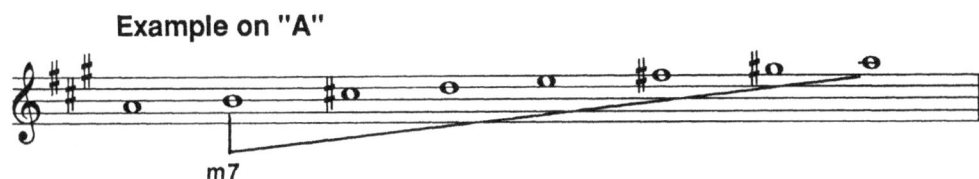

Compose a **four measure phrase, emphasizing** the **minor 7th.**

EXAMPLE:

OCTAVE   - (8va)

The **interval** of the **Octave** occurs **between** the **following notes** of the **major scale:**

Example on "C"

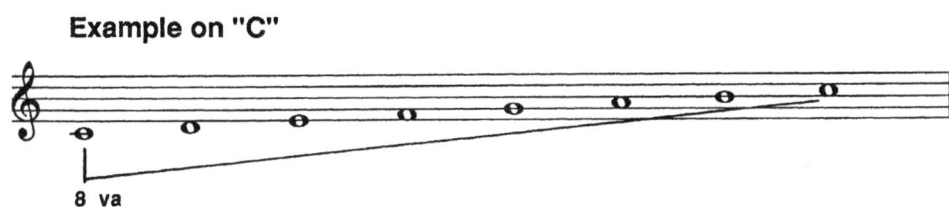

Compose a **four measure phrase, emphasizing** the **Octave.**

EXAMPLE:

UNEVEN PHRASING

Up **to this point** all **phrases have been even** - two or four measures (the most commonly used in popular music). However, **uneven phrases may also be used**: **Ex. one - three measures**. **Remember**, phrases are **arbitrary divisions of notes into cohesive, understandable units** (clause or sentences in literature), which **come together** creating a **complete musical thought**.

ONE MEASURE PHRASE (FRAGMENT)

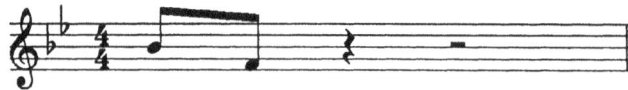

THREE MEASURE PHRASE

FIVE MEASURE PHRASE

CHAPTER III

THE MOTIF - MOTIVE

This is a **musical statement, fragment, or phrase*** which may be **developed** into a **complete thought** using the techniques discussed in this chapter.

EXAMPLE OF BASIC MOTIF

ONE MEASURE MOTIF   TWO MEASURE MOTIF

DEVELOPMENT OF BASIC MOTIF

A) **REPETITION:** Repeating a motif or phrase either exactly or with a slight variation of melody or rhythm. The repetition doesn't have to follow exactly, but can be played at various points during a musical composition, to help unify all the different elements.

MOTIF   EXACT REPETITION

MOTIF   SLIGHT VARIATION

*A motif, usually a brief statement, may be any length you wish - Ex. 2, 3, 4 measures etc.

B) **SEQUENCE:** In this technique the motif's interval pattern is played starting on a different note, imitating the original idea, only on a different plane (level). The sequence may be rhythmically exact or varied. If only the number (4th, 5th, 6th, etc.) of the interval is imitated, you'll remain in the same key.

MOTIF   SEQUENCE   SEQUENCE

5th 2nd   2nd 2nd   5th 2nd   2nd 2nd

However, if the quality (major - minor - dim. - aug.) of the interval is also imitated, a key change will occur. If done correctly, this is a valuable technique.

MOTIF   SEQUENCE

P 5   M 2   M 2   m 2   P 5   M 2   M 2   m 2

MOTIF   SEQUENCE WITH VARIATION

C) **AUGMENTATION:** The motif may be altered by doubling the time value of each note.

MOTIF   AUGMENTATION

D) **DIMINUTION:** The motif may be altered by decreasing the time value of each note by half (the most common).

MOTIF   DIMINUTION

E) RANDOM RHYTHMIC VARIATION: Altering the original motif by randomly changing the time value of each note.

MOTIF   RANDOM VARIATION

F) RETROGRADE: In this technique the notes of the original idea will be played backwards with or without variation.

MOTIF   RETROGRADE EXACT   RETROGRADE VARIED

G) INVERSION: To invert a phrase or motif, you start on the same tone, keeping the same interval distance*, but reversing the direction. Again, the inversion may be rhythmically exact or with variation.

MOTIF   INVERSION

INVERSION WITH VARIATION

H) FRAGMENTATION AND EXTENSION: In this technique, a group of notes from the end of the motif is developed and extended.

FRAGMENTATION AND EXTENSION

I) SILENCE: A pause at the right moment can be as effective as any musical statement.

*The same rules apply here as with the sequence. If just the numeral distance is used, the key will stay the same. However, if the quality is also used, a key change will take place.

STUDENT EXERCISES

We'll now develop **two bar phrases** *into* **six bar groupings** by applying the techniques we have studied.

A) **REPETITION**
B) **SEQUENCE**
C) **AUGMENTATION**
D) **DIMINUTION**
E) **RANDOM RHYTHMIC VARIATION**
F) **RETROGRADE**
G) **INVERSION**
H) **SILENCE**

Develop your original motif (2 measures) into six measures by using the following examples as guideline:

A.   REPETITION: Repeat the motif either exactly or with variation.

B.   SEQUENCE :   Sequences of the original motif with or without variation.

Combining repetition and sequence with or without variation.

Connect one or both phrases with connecting tones.

MOTIF   CONNECTING TONES   SEQUENCE

MOTIF

C.   AUGMENTATION: Augmentation of the original motif with or without variation.

MOTIF   AUGMENTATION

D.   DIMINUTION: Diminution of the original motif with or without variation. Of course you may combine the various techniques.

MOTIF   SEQUENCE+ DIMINUTION   SEQUENCE

SEQUENCE+ DIMINUTION

E.   RANDOM RHYTHMIC VARIATION: Variation of rhythm with original motif or sequence.

MOTIF   CONNECTING TONES   SEQUENCE VARIED   CON.TONES
                        3   3

MOTIF VARIED

F.   RETROGRADE: Retrograde of original motif with or without variation.

G.   INVERSION: Invert original motif with or without variation.

H.   FRAGMENTATION: Fragment and develop the end of the motif.

All of these techniques may be combined in any order you wish to develop a motif. However, it's very important to remember that <u>these are only guidelines</u>. You're free to let your ear, personal creativity, and taste lead the motif in any direction you wish - *you are the creator* - the artist.

CHAPTER IV

EIGHT MEASURES

We're now going to **enlarge our writing** from **six to eight measures**. There are an **endless variety of ways** modern composers **accomplish this**. We're going to study some of the most commonly used methods from popular literature as well as some original examples. **Imitating the form, style, and techniques of others will help you develop your own style.**

A **group of phrases** combined to **form eight measures** is called a **"section"**. Later on these sections will be given **letter names** (A-B-C-D, etc.) to **show their location** in a song.

The following **examples illustrate how** the **7th and 8th measures** either **end the section, pause** for a moment, **lead back to the beginning** of that section, or **lead to a new** section. Use these examples as **guides** to **create your own 8 measure sections, combining** the **6 measures** you've already developed **with the 7th and 8th measure techniques** now introduced.

STUDENT EXERCISES

<u>COMPOSE EIGHT MEASURE SECTIONS USING:</u>

1. The tonic **held over the 7th and 8th measures** will bring the **section** to a **definite end.**

EXAMPLE:

The **5th and 6th measures** will be **one short phrase** *leading* to the tonic which will be **sustained over** the **7th and 8th measures.** This will **end the 8 measures.**

Use the examples as guides for your own exercises as far as key, phrasing, time signature, and style are concerned.

2. A **scale tone**, <u>other</u> <u>than</u> the tonic, held **over the 7th and 8th measures** creating a **pause**.

EXAMPLE:

3. A **phrase** in the **7th and 8th measures** that **leads** us **to the beginning of the section** (a *"turnaround"* phrase).

EXAMPLE:

4. A **phrase** in the **7th and 8th measures** that **ends** the **section**.

EXAMPLE:

*Repeat signs - repeat to the beginning.

5. A **phrase** in the **7th and 8th measures** which creates a **pause**.

EXAMPLE:

6. A **phrase** in the **7th and 8th measures** that **leads** us to a **new section**.

EXAMPLE:

NOTE: Throughout the history of music, composers in all styles of music, have analyzed the works of others for inspiration. You should look at as many songs as possible to see how sections are formed - sequences, repetitions, phrase lengths, endings, pauses, etc. You can never stop learning from others.

The **following songs** from popular literature **contain 8 bar opening sections. All examples quoted** from literature **will be from John Lennon** and **Paul McCartney.** I've done this for the following reasons:

A. The **vast amount** of musical examples to call upon.

B. They're the **Masters** of modern songwriting.

C. You can **easily find** all the examples in print and on records. If you don't own the materials, your local library should contain all the examples mentioned.

D. Their music will **never** go out of style.

E. It will be much easier for you to go to **one source** rather than many.

"ALL MY LOVING"   "LOVE OF THE LOVED"   "RINGO'S THEME"   "FROM A WINDOW"   "I DON'T WANT TO SEE YOU AGAIN"   "I'LL FOLLOW THE SUN" "LIKE DREAMERS DO"   "IF I NEEDED SOMEONE"   "NOWHERE MAN"   "GOT TO GET YOU INTO MY LIFE"   "FOR NO ONE"   "YOU NEVER GIVE ME YOUR MONEY" "LUCY IN THE SKY WITH DIAMONDS"   "P.S. I LOVE YOU"

CHAPTER V

MELODY AND CHORDS

In most musical forms, the **melody and chords** <u>interact</u> <u>with</u> and <u>reflect</u> each other. An accomplished musician can *"hear"* which chords will **enhance** a given melody. **The reverse** of this is **also true**. Many composers will play various chords and progressions **"hearing"** (forming in their minds) many different melodies. The **first book in this series**, *"Chords and Progressions"*, **deals with hearing melodies as chords are played.** The **interplay** of **chord** and **scale tones** <u>create</u> melody. The **notes** generally **emphasized*** in any given **measure** are those **corresponding** to the **chord being played.** (Chord Construction - pg. 65.)

In the following well known melody, **"Amazing Grace"**, the **number** <u>under</u> each **note shows** its **relationship** to the **corresponding chord.** The **chord symbol** (Ex. - C for C Major) is shown **above** each **measure** and is **also written out below** with the **chord tones numbered.** [The **chords** are **written** in the **treble clef** and in the **tonic position** to make it **easier to see the relationship** of the **melody note to the chord tones.**] **Study these relationships** by **playing** and **singing** each example so you can **hear and feel each note sounding against the chord.** If you're **not familiar with chords and keys**, that *<u>will</u> <u>not</u>* **stop you** from **completing this book.** As stated in the Introduction, this **book deals ONLY** with **melody** constructed from **scale material.** I've **inserted** this section at this point *ONLY* to **show you** the **relationship of the chords and melody** and **where to look for their explanation.**

*An emphasized tone is any note on which a phrase may start, pause, or end.

**CT = chord tone.   ST = scale tone.

AMAZING GRACE

G MAJOR SCALE   KEY OF G*

G   Am   Bm   C   D   Em   F#dim.

Chord Tone**

*Major Keys - See Pg. 63.
**See Pg. 65.

SCALE AND CHORD TONE RELATIONSHIPS

You should **study the relationship** of a particular **note or notes sounding against** a **given chord** or **progression** in order to create **interesting and memorable melodies**. Most **composers create songs** by **using either or both of the following methods:**

MELODIC DEVELOPMENT: The melody is conceived in a **horizontal (↔) direction** with the <u>emphasis</u> **placed** on **melodic development** using the techniques we've been studying up to this point. That melody is then **harmonized** with **chords** that *enhance* and *compliment* it.

CHORD PROGRESSION: In this style of composition the composer **creates** or **adapts** a **standard progression* first** and then, using a <u>mixture</u> of chords and non-harmonic **tones****, creates (hears) a **melody**. **Unlimited melodies** can be **created against any given chord progression.**

8 MEASURE CHORD PROGRESSION

We'll now **compose** <u>different</u> **8 measure sections** using the **notes** of each chord **combined** with the **non-chord tones.**

Each exercise will **introduce a new technique** with an **explanation and example** of **how to use it in composing.** The **notes** of each chord **are shown in the progression** so you can see at a glance **which notes to work with.**

BASIC PROGRESSION

*Chord progressions can't be copyrighted. Ex. - Blues Progression.
**Chord construction (Pg. 65) Non-harmonic tones are introduced and explained in this Chapter.
***Chord tones will be shown in their closest position. If you prefer you can, of course, use any octave.

COMPOSE A MELODY TO THE BASIC PROGRESSION USING:

1. **Only the notes of each chord** as that chord is played. **Rhythmic originality** can make your **solos interesting**, even with the limited material you have to work with. **Remember** to **phrase properly.**

EXAMPLE:

Cmaj7   Fmaj7

2. **Passing Tones (Diatonic):** These are the **scale tones** of the **key you're in** played <u>between</u> the **chord tones.** Our **examples are in the key of C Major.**

EXAMPLE:

Cmaj7   Fmaj7

3. **Appoggiatura:** These are (usually) the scale tones **above** the **chord tones** played on a **strong beat*** and then **resolving** (*moving to*) the **chord tone below it.** This generally produces a very expressive coloring.

EXAMPLE:

Cmaj7   Fmaj7

App.   C.T   App.   C.T   App.   C.T   C.T.

The **Appoggiatura** may also be **below the chord tone.** In this case it **can be a half-tone below** the chord tone, **even if it's not in the key.**

EXAMPLE:

Cmaj7   Fmaj7

App.   C.T.   P.T.   C.T.   C.T.   App.   C.T.

At this point you should combine the passing tones and Appoggiatura with the chord tones. After each technique is introduced, combine it with the ones previously learned.

*1st and 3rd beat in 4/4 time - 1st beat in 3/4 time.

The **Appoggiatura** also may be a **whole tone below the chord tone** *if* <u>in the scale</u>.

EXAMPLE:

Cmaj.7   Fmaj.7

App.   C.T.   C.T.   C.T   C.T.   App.   C.T.   C.T..

4. **Suspension:** The suspension is basically the same as the Appoggiatura **except** it is a **note in one chord** which is **sustained** (held over) **as the chord changes,** and then **resolves to a chord tone of the new chord.**

EXAMPLE: Suspended notes resolving **downward.**

Cmaj.7   Fmaj.7

Susp. Resolution

EXAMPLE: Suspended notes resolving **upward.**

Cmaj.7   Fmaj.7

C.T.   C.T.   P.T.   C.T.   Susp.   Resolution

33

5. **Anticipation:** This may be thought of as **the opposite of suspension.** While one chord is **sounding,** a note **from the next chord** is **played** *just before that note is sounded* - thereby **creating the anticipation.**

EXAMPLE:

6. **Auxiliary Tone:** This is a **note** which is usually **one scale tone above or one half-step below** a chord tone. The **chord tone** is played **first,** followed by the **auxiliary note** and then the **chord again.**

EXAMPLE:

7. **Chromatic Passing Tones:** These may be used **between** chord tones, but care must be taken **not to overdo** this technique. In the **proper place,** and used **sparingly,** the **effect** can be **very interesting. Overdone** it will sound **old-fashioned** and **dated.**

EXAMPLE:

8. **Delayed Resolutions of Non-Chord Tones:** The **movement** of a **non-chord** to a **chord tone** may be **delayed** by the **addition** of **one or more notes** *before* the **resolution.** The **following examples illustrate this technique.**

EXAMPLE:

It's very **important to remember** that a **good melody** will **contain many colors** - like an interesting work of art. **Tension and release** (calm) are two **very important qualities** in **creating these colors**. The **following chart lists** some of the way **tension and release** can be **created:**

<table>
<tr><td><u>TENSION</u></td><td><u>RELEASE</u></td></tr>
<tr><td>*DISSONANCE (Emphasis of non-chord and sale tones)</td><td>*CONSONANCE (Emphasis on scale and cho</td></tr>
<tr><td>*ACCELERATING RHYTHMS</td><td>*CONSONANT INTERVALS</td></tr>
<tr><td>*CONTINUING REPETITIONS</td><td>*LONG FLOWING PHRASES</td></tr>
<tr><td>*DISSONANT INTERVALS</td><td>*NO SUDDEN CHANGES IN</td></tr>
<tr><td>*DISJOINTED RHYTHMS</td><td>   RHYTHM OR DYNAMICS</td></tr>
<tr><td>*FRAGMENTED MOTIFS</td><td>*COMPLETE IDEAS</td></tr>
<tr><td>*UNEXPECTED MOTION</td><td>*EXPECTED MOTION</td></tr>
<tr><td>*UNEXPECTED DYNAMICS</td><td>*LACK OF DYNAMICS</td></tr>
</table>

NOTE: Dynamics, so often forgotten, **can make an <u>average</u> melody into a *great* one.**

You should always **search** for **new and interesting chord progressions**, and then <u>**write**</u> as many **melodies** as possible **to each progression**.

****

CHAPTER VI

"A SECTIONS" OF VARYING LENGTHS

Eight measure sections, although very **common**, <u>are</u> <u>not</u> the only ones used. These **sections may be composed** of **any number of measures and phrases**. When one of these sections **introduces** the **first theme of a song**, it is called the **"A Section"**.

There are **many ways** of **composing "A Sections"** of **varying length. Listed below** are some of the **most commonly used methods:**

1. Take an **eight measure section** and **make it longer** by **adding** one or more **measures** which **delay the entrance** of the **next section**, or a **return to the beginning of that section**. This **creates tension** which will *build* until the **entrance of the next section**. As stated before - **music must balance tension and calm** to be **interesting**.

EXAMPLE: 9 MEASURES

EXTENDED-9 BARS

EXAMPLE: 10 measures

2. **Write** a **shorter section** - *or* - **shorten** an **existing section one or more measures.**

EXAMPLE:

3. **Develop your original ideas into 12 or 16** (or any number you'd like) **measures** rather than stopping at 8. You can also **alter the even 12 or 16 measure sections** to **uneven groupings** by **adding or subtracting measures** as we did with the 8 bar sections.

EXAMPLE:

NOTE: Since most listeners (consciously or subconsciously) will **perceive the irregular sectioning** as **something different**, the *effect* should be a **sense of added interest** which will make your composition **memorable**.

Now we'll **compose "A Sections" of varying lengths** using **famous melodies as guides** (blueprints). **Imitate the length, phrasing, repetition, sequences, etc. Create your <u>own</u> "A Sections". DO NOT COPY** - only <u>**IMITATE**</u> the form. You can always learn from the great composers.

When **analyzing a section** to **imitate its form**, remember to **look for the following:**

A) **Length of Section**
B) **Number of Phrases**
C) **Length of Phrases**
D) **Motif Development through Repetitions, Sequence, etc.**
E) **Principal Rhythms Used**
F) **General Tempo and Feel of Section - General Mood of Piece**
G) **Chord Progression - Type of Chords Used**

CHAPTER VII

ANALYZATION

The following is an **example** of how an **"A Section"** should be **analyzed**:

1)   **Key - E Major**
2)   **12 Bars long with a pick-up.**
3)   **Three - four bar phrases**
4)   **1st phrase (motif) end with a pause on 5th of scale.**
5)   **2nd phrase - repeated 1st phrase with a pause on 3rd of scale.**
6)   **3rd phrase - repeated 1st phrase but ends on tonic against I chord.**

Medium rock tempo. Mostly non-syncopated. Basic chords in rock idiom.

EXAMPLE

Compose "A Sections" using these songs as guidelines:

1) **"Love Me Do"** by John Lennon and Paul McCartney. The **"A Section"** of this song is **13 measures** long. It is **divided into 6 phrases**.

2) **"I Saw Her Standing There"** by Lennon - McCartney. The **"A Section"** is **16 measures** long **divided into 5 phrases**.

3) **"Yesterday"** by Lennon - McCartney. The **"A Section"** is **7 measures** long **divided into 4 phrases**.

The **following songs** also use **"A Sections"** of **varying lengths**:

"Do You Want to Know a Secret"	**14 bars**
"And I Love Her"	**10 bars**
"I Want to Hold Your Hand"	**12 bars**

CHAPTER VIII

"A SECTIONS" IN MINOR*

"A Sections" based on <u>minor</u> scales will be treated exactly as those based on major.

Melodies derived from minor scales are very common in all styles of modern composition. However, the harmonic and natural minor scales are used more often than the melodic because of their construction. Pay *particular attention* to the intervals created - they may be awkward and difficult to sing. <u>Your hearing should be the final judge</u>.

EXERCISES:

Compose "A Sections" of varying length using the following scales. The following examples should serve as guides ONLY.

A minor -natural

1   A MINOR - NATURAL

EX.

D- HARMONIC MINOR

2   D MINOR - HARMONIC

EX.

*For a complete explanation and list of minor scales, see Page 66 - Minor Key Construction.

#3   E MINOR - MELODIC

EX.

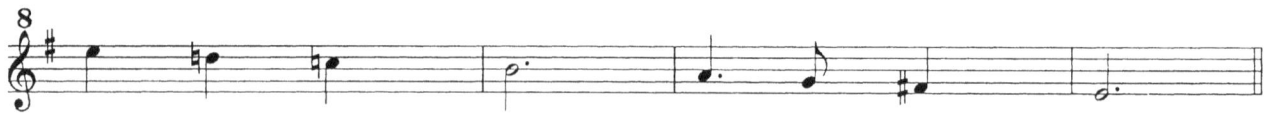

#4   B MINOR - NATURAL

EX.

#5   G MINOR - HARMONIC

EX.

The following **excerpts** from **popular literature** use the **minor scales**.

GREENSLEEVES

ALL THROUGH THE NIGHT

The following **Beatle songs** are in the **minor mode**:

"AND I LOVE HER"

"THINGS WE SAID TODAY"

"ELEANOR RIGBY"

"HAPPINESS IS A WARM GUN"

CHAPTER IX

WORDS (LYRICS) AND MELODY (COMBINED)

Up to this point you've been composing melodies of varying lengths. Now you'll **start combining words and melodies**. There are basically **two methods of doing this**:

1. **Melody first** - the music is composed first, as you've been doing, followed by lyrics which are made to fit the melody*

2. **Lyrics first** - a specific text (poem or story) is set to music in a way that makes sense and "gets across" the meaning, feel, and style of the words. **Sentence structure must be carefully considered**.

In order to **gain experience** in **both** ways of combining lyrics and melody - and at the same time **see how famous composers accomplished this** - use the following **procedure**:

    A. Rewrite the **first 4 measures** (melody) to *fit* the **words of the song**.

EXAMPLE: **AMAZING GRACE**

ORIGINAL

A   maz- ing-   Grace! How   sweet the   sound that

KEEP ORIGINAL WORDS - WRITE NEW MELODY TO FIT.

NEW MELODY

A-   maz- ing-   Grace! How   sweet the   sound that

*Remember, each syllable will have one note, or you can hold the syllable for two, three, four, or more notes. There's no hard and fast rule.

B. Rewrite the **lyrics** of the **1st four measures** to *fit* the **melody.**

ORIGINAL MELODY

It seems to- me that love is blind when

NEW WORDS

C. Combine your melody and words.

NEW MELODY

It seems to- me that love is blind when

NEW WORDS

KEEP IN MIND, WE STUDY AND ANALYZE THE WORKS OF OTHERS TO LEARN AND GROW MUSICALLY - *NOT TO COPY OR PLAGIARIZE.*

Rewrite an **excerpt** from **popular music** using the techniques you've just learned:

    A) **Rewrite** <u>melody</u> **to fit the words**
    b) **Rewrite** <u>words</u> **to fit the melody**
    C) **Combine** your **new words and melody**

As stated previously, **this exercise will help you capture the "feel and style"** of varied successful songwriters. Combined with the knowledge you've acquired, this will give you the **foundation to write in any idiom or style.**

Keep in mind that **a well written song** is **phrased** so that **breaths are taken in a natural manner** without disrupting the flow the song. **The two and four-bar phrases** are <u>only guidelines</u>. **There are no absolutes.** Each part of the phrase can vary, depending on what you're trying to say.

CHAPTER X

A¹ · A² SECTIONS

In most instances **popular songs** will **repeat the "A Section"**, either exactly or with some slight variations. The **first section** will be **called "A¹"** and the **second "A²"**. The **repetition** of sections **make the song understandable** and **memorable**. The **words** (lyrics) are **usually different** in the **A² section**. The **A²** section can **be written out** or you can **use repeat signs** (EXPLAINED FURTHER ON THE FOLLOWING PAGE) with the **second set** of **words underneath the first**.

EXAMPLE:

A¹ · A² - Same melody. 8 measures - repeated exactly with different words.

It's **common practice**, when **repeating section**s, to have a **different ending** for **each section**. At the **end** of the **1st section** (A¹) the first ending will **contain a note or notes** that **tell the listener** that this **section will be repeated** - in other words, the **1st ending** will **bring us back** to the **beginning**. At the **end of the 2nd section** (A²) the **tonic may** be used to **bring** this **section** to a **definite end** - preparing the listener for something new - or a phrase which **will lead us back again. Instead of** *rewriting* the **section in full again**, <u>"1st"</u> and <u>"2nd"</u> **endings may be used.**

STUDENT EXERCISES

Compose A¹ · A² sections using your **previously written "A Sections":**

By **altering** the **last measures, create A¹ · A²** sections. The **end of the A¹ section** should **contain a scale tone which creates a pause** or **scale tones which create a phrase, both** of which **return** us to the **beginning**. The **A² section** should <u>either</u> come **to a definite end with** the **tonic against the I chord** <u>or</u> **a phrase which introduces** the **next section to follow.**

Study the following **examples** which **illustrate how** the **A¹** and **A² sections are** the **same** with **different endings.**

The **following Beatle songs** use the A[1] · A[2] **format** in the <u>beginning</u> of the **song:**

"AND I LOVE HER"

"RINGO'S THEME"

"YESTERDAY"

"FOR NO ONE"

"B" SECTION

Now that you've **composed** the **A¹ · A²** sections, you **must add one more section** to **complete** the **most basic form** (structure) in **popular music - A¹ · A² · B · A²**. This **new section** (**B*** - **Bridge**) for the *time being* will be **related to the "A Section"** in **scale, form, feel, time,** and **rhythm.** We will study later on how this may be altered.

A **"B" section** is simply a **new section to add variety.** It **usually starts on a chord**, such as the IV chord, which **immediately gives** the **impression of something new**. The **end** of the **"B" section ends with** a **phrase and chord** which **returns** us to the **beginning** of the "A **Section".**

You should **compose this "B"** section in **exactly** the **same way** you **composed the other sections.**

LEADS BACK TO THE BEGINNING

Compose B sections to your **already written A¹ · A² sections.** Remember, **lead away from** and **then return to** your **A sections.**

*B is not an abbreviation for bridge. Each new added section will be given a letter name, i.e.: A - B - C - D - etc.

A¹ · A² · B · A²

It is *important* that the **B section lead away from**, and **then back to**, the **A² section**. This will **complete** the **A¹ · A² · B · A² structure** (the most basic of all popular song forms). The **A² section** is used **after the bridge** because it **has a definite ending**, which first **prepared** the **listener for the bridge**, and **will** now **end the song**.

A¹ · A² · B · A² SONG EXAMPLES

A¹ – this will contain the chords of the first eight measures. Compose the melody and words to go with these chords. The chords given, along with your melody and words, should bring you to the A² section.

A² – the chords and melody of this section will be the same as A¹, except it should have different words, and it should come to a definite end.

B – the chords of the "bridge" will be different from the "A" section. Your melody and words should be different, but related, to the "A" section in style and feel. Try to make the end of the bridge lead back to "A²."

A² – the end of the song. It will be a repeat of the A² section, with its definite end, but with different words.

Ex. #1: A¹

Now that she's gone I am here all a - lone, And I sit by my - self, Just__ wait-ing for the dawn.

Ex. #2: A²

Sky is all dark, and the stars do not shine, My__ love's gone a - way And__ broke my heart this day.

Ex. #3: B

We had a love so true I thought it nev-er end Now she's found some-one new, That's when my life did end so, .

Ex. #4: A²

Here I do sit, In the gloom of the night Just__ dream-ing of her And__ wait-ing for the dawn.

Another **example** of the <u>**A-A-B-A**</u> **form** is:

YESTERDAY
by Lennon and McCartney

A¹	7 measures
A²	A¹ repeated exactly
Bridge	8 measures (4 bar phrase repeated twice)
A²	Repeated exactly (last 2 bars repeated for ending)

CHAPTER XI

VARIATIONS IN FORM

Even though $A^1 \cdot A^2 \cdot B \cdot A^2$ is the foundation, and for many years the standard, it is not the only song form used. Modern composers not only vary the number of measures in a section (6 - 7 - 8 - 9 etc.), but the number of sections (A - B - C - D, etc.) and their function in the overall composition. The following are the most commonly used sections which combine to create endless varieties to your song.

INTRODUCTION (Intro)

A short instrumental section (usually 4 to 8 measures) that introduces the "A Section". The background (instrumental accompaniment) of the intro is usually the same as that of the "A Section" . A short introductory motif may also be used.

HOOK

This section, usually 8 bars long, is repeated over and over - creating a hypnotic effect with its constant repetition. It is very common for the hook to be introduced after a fairly long "A Section" and before the bridge.

INTERLUDE

This is an instrumental section placed in the middle of a song added for variety. It may be written out or improvised, depending on the style of music. In jazz and some forms of rock, these interludes are improvised and may be quite long. The interlude may use the chords to one of the song's sections or be completely independent.

In the performance or recording of most songs, a short instrumental solo (again - usually improvised) is added, replacing the words to a certain section. This is known by various names, i.e.: solo, riff, jazz chorus, ride, etc.

CODA

The coda (tail) is an extra - or added - ending.   EXAMPLE: The end of "Michelle"

VERSE

The section of the song that gives the impression of an ongoing story or poem over a repeated melody.

CHORUS (Refrain)

Words and music repeated EXACTLY after one or more verses are sung. The verse and chorus style is common in traditional folk music.

The **following original song** is **analyzed** to **show** you **how** a **complete modern song** is **constructed** with **various sections** and their **repeats.**

INTRO - 11 measures
A¹ - 18 measures
A² - 19 measures
B - (HOOK) The **B section** will **serve as the hook** in this song - **8 measures -**
repeated
C - (BRIDGE) - 12 measures

The **form** (order of sections) **will be:**

Intro - A¹ - A² - B - C - A² - B - B - B etc.

(ORIGINAL SONG)

52

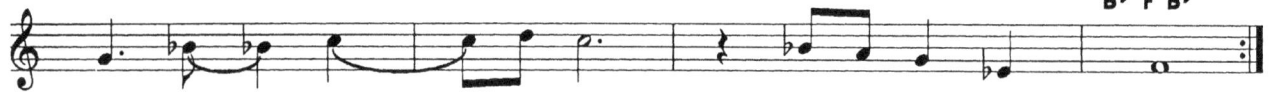

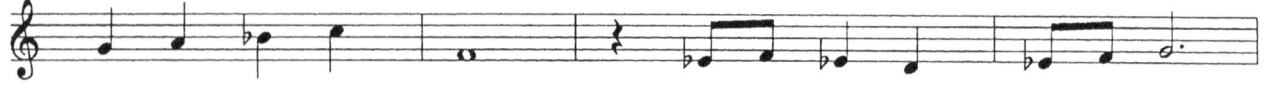

Most modern **composers** **use** an **Intro** plus 3 sections of **varying** **lengths**. They can **create** many **different** **forms** by how the **sections** **are** **repeated** and **in** **what** **order**. **Listed** **below** are some **typical** **examples**. **Remember**, the **hook** **is** **usually** **repeated over and over** at the **end** **of** the song.

1   Intro - A¹ - A² - B - A¹ - A² (Instrumental) - B - A² - Coda

2   Intro - A¹ - A² - B - Intro - A¹ - A² - B - Intro (Intro acts as ending)

3   Intro - A - Interlude - B (Hook) - A - Interlude - B - A - Interlude - B - B - B etc.

4   Intro - A¹ - A² - B - Intro - A² - Interlude - A² - Interlude (Short Instrumental) - C (Hook) - Intro - A² - Interlude - C - C - C etc.

5   Intro - A¹ - A² - B (Hook) - A² - B - C - A² - B - B - B etc.

6   Intro - A¹ - A² - B - C (Hook) - A¹ - A² - B - C - C - C etc.

7   Intro - A - B - A - B - A (Instrumental) - Intro

8   Intro - A - B (Hook) - Intro - A - B - C - A - B - B - B - B etc.

9   Intro - A - B - Intro - A - B - Intro - A - B - Intro (Repeat over and over)

#10   Intro - A¹ - A² - B (Hook) - A² - B - C - A - B - B - B etc.

#11   Intro - A - B - C (Hook) - Intro - A - B - C - Intro - B - C - C - C etc.

You can see that **there are endless ways** in which **sections** **can be grouped** to **form** a **complete thought**. **Form** is essential in making a song both **interesting and memorable**. The **different sections** are **for variety** and the **repetition for memorability**. **Continuous repetition**, such as the **hook**, **has a hypnotizing effect on the listener** and is the **part** that is **most remembered**. The **amount of sections** you use **is entirely up to you** - there are no restrictions.

The following **Lennon and McCartney selections** are **analyzed** to **show how** these great **songs were constructed:**

"A DAY IN THE LIFE"

SECTIONS:

Intro = 4 bars · A^1 = 10 bars · A^2 = 9 bars · A^3 = 12 bars · Interlude = 11 bars · B = 11 bars · C = 10 bars ·

FORM:

Intro · A^1 · A^2 · A^3 · Interlude · B · C · A^2 (Extended with part of A^3 to build up tension until the final chord is sounded.

"WITH A LITTLE HELP FROM MY FRIENDS"

SECTIONS:

Intro = 4 bars · A = 8 bars ·   B = 8 bars (Hook) · C = 8 bars (Bridge) · Coda = Same as B only extended.

FORM:

Intro · A · B · A · B · C · A · B · C · B extended

"LUCY IN THE SKY WITH DIAMONDS"

SECTIONS:

Intro = 4 bars · A = 16 bars (Extended) · B = 13 bars · C = 7 bars (Hook) ·   Coda (Hook)

FORM:

A · B · C · A · B · C · A · C (Repeat and Fade)

"ELEANOR RIGBY"

SECTIONS:

Intro = 8 bars · A = 10 bars · B = 8 bars

FORM:

Intro · A · B · A · B · Intro · A · B · Coda

"HERE, THERE, EVERYWHERE"

SECTIONS:
Intro = 3 bars   ·   A = 8 bars   ·   B = 4 bars

FORM:
Intro · A · A · B · A · B · A (Last A extended 4 bars to end)

"AND I LOVE HER"

SECTIONS:
Intro = 4 bars   ·   A = 10 bars   ·   B = 8 bars

FORM:
Repeats = Intro · A · A · B · A · A (Instrumental) ·   A ·   Intro used as ending

"IMAGINE"

SECTIONS:
Intro = 4 bars   ·   A = 12 bars   ·   B = 8 bars

FORM:
Repeats = Intro · A · A · B · A · B

"YESTERDAY"

SECTIONS:
Intro = 2 bars   ·   A = 7 bars   ·   B = 8 bars

FORM:
Intro · A · A · B · A · B ·   A (Last A extended by repeating last 2 bars)

"MICHELLE"

SECTIONS:
Intro = 4 bars · A = 6 bars · B = 10 bars

FORM:
Intro · A · A · B · A · B · A (Instrumental) · B · A (Extended to 11 bars with added section - closing section)

CLOSING STATEMENT

We've studied the most common methods of creating music in the modern song style. These techniques apply to all styles and forms of musical composition.

Let the end of this book be the beginning of an unending journey of musical creation. Keep expanding the knowledge of your mind and the boundaries of your imagination.

MAJOR SCALES

The Major Scales are the basic building blocks used in writing popular music. These are the tools in creating your own songs. The scales are built on a specific number of half and whole steps. A half step occurs when two tones are directly next to each other.

Ex. #1:

A whole step is two consecutive half or semi-tones.

Ex. #2:

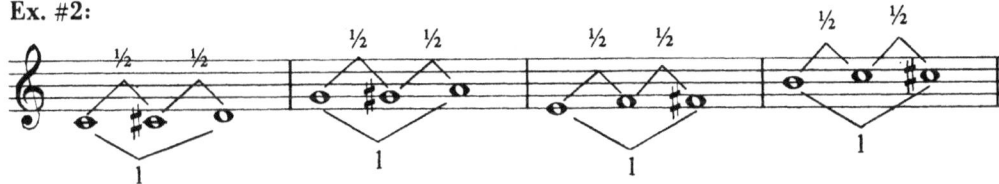

The Major Scales are composed of the specific order of whole-whole-half-whole-whole-whole-half steps (1-1-½-1-1-1-½). This is called Diatonic.

Ex. #3:
C Major Scale

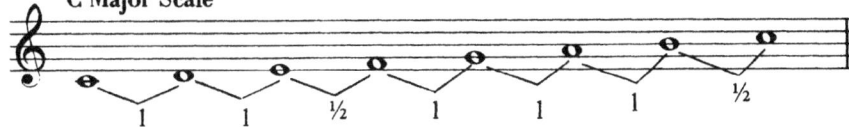

Ex. #4:
G Major Scale

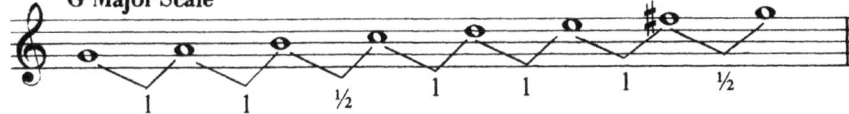

Ex. #5:
F Major Scale

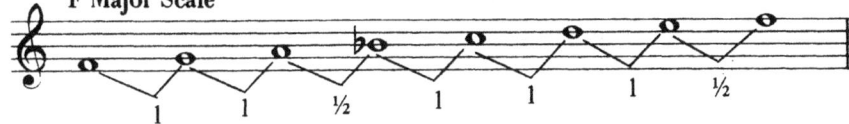

58

You should make every endeavor to memorize these scales, as you will be using and referring to them in this book constantly.

MAJOR SCALES

The sharps or flats of each scale placed in front of the staff is the key signature. It tells you what notes are to be ♯ or ♭ in the song.

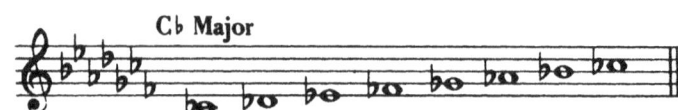

KEY SIGNATURES

CYCLE OF 5ths

The cycle of 5th's is a chart illustrating the Diatonic Major Scales and their sharps or flats (Key Signatures).

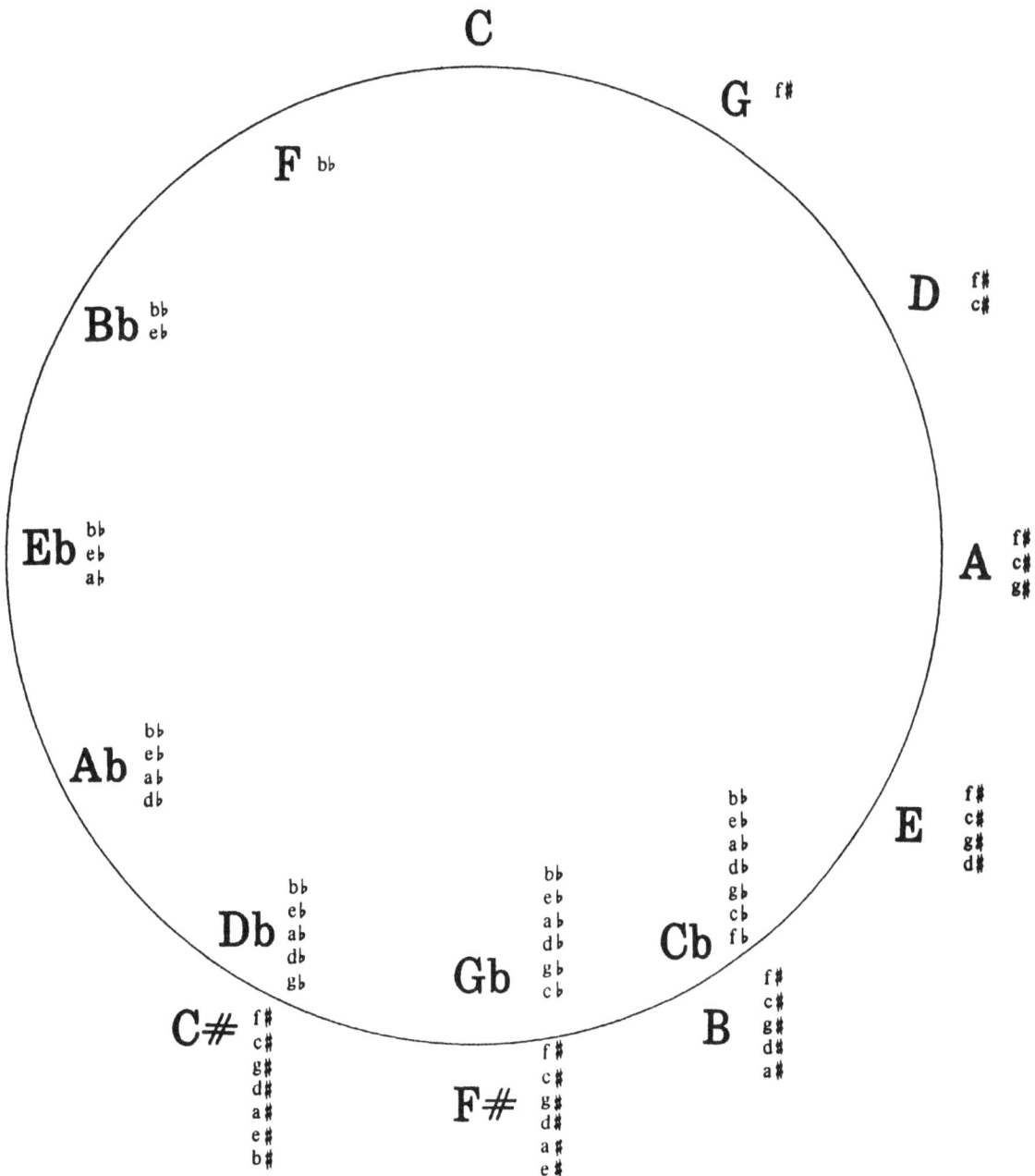

INTERVALS

The **distance between two notes** is **called** an **interval**. The **distance** is **calculated by** the **number** of **diatonic scale tones** <u>between</u> the two notes.

The **intervals** are also **given names** to **determine** the **number of half-steps** (Pg. 57) **contained between them**:

Ex. - Major 2nd = 2 half-steps, Major 3rd = 5 half-steps, Major 6th = 10 half-steps.

*Latin word for "eight".

Listed **below** are the **most commonly used methods** of **determining** these **names**:

"MAJOR": When **referring to a 2nd - 3rd - 6th - or 7th** interval, the **term major is used** when the **higher** of the **two tones** is **in the major scale of** the **lower note**.

EXAMPLES

M2-up   M3-up   M6-down   M7-down

"MINOR": When the **upper note** is **one-half step** <u>below</u> **major**, it is called minor.

EXAMPLES

m2-up   m3-up   m6-down   m7-down

"PERFECT": If the **higher tone** is **in the scale** of the **lower**, the **interval of the 4th, 5th, or octave** it is called **"perfect"**.

EXAMPLES

P4-up   P5-up   P4-down   P5-down

"DIMINISHED": **One half-step** <u>below</u> **perfect** or **minor** is **"diminished"**.

EXAMPLES

Dim.4-up   Dim.5-up   Dim.5-down   Dim.4-down

"AUGMENTED":   **One half-step <u>above</u> major** or perfect **is "augmented"**.

EXAMPLES

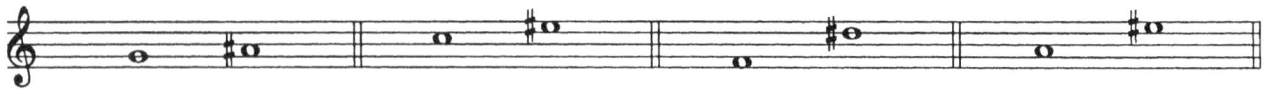

Aug.2-up   Aug.3-up   Aug.6-up   Aug.5-up

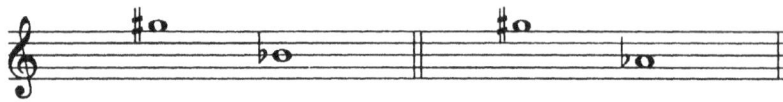

Aug.6-down   Aug.7-down

MAJOR KEYS

The Major Keys are families of chords interacting upon each other. Their movement and qualities create the basics for harmony. There are fifteen (15) Major Keys. They are based on the fifteen (15) major scales.

Ex. #1.

Key of C Major

1. First you must write the major scale of the key you want.

2. Upon each note of the major scale, build a triad.

3. Number the triads with Roman numerals from I to VII. The 8th chord is the same as the first, and since the octave does not matter in the key construction, it is eliminated for now.

I	II	III	IV	V	VI	VII
C	Dm	Em	F	G	Am	B°

4. Label the chords by referring to the chart of chords.

5. These are the chords in the key.

6. The pattern that emerges from the creating of triads on each scale tone will be the same for all fifteen (15) Major Keys.

7. All I chords will be Major.
   All II chords will be minor.
   All III chords will be minor.
   All IV chords will be Major.
   All V chords will be Major.
   All VI chords will be minor.
   All VII chords will be diminished.

64

CHORDS

Chords are the combination of 3 or more different tones sounding together. These chords are derived from the Major Scales. The 7th, 9th, 11th, and 13th chords are extensions of the four basic types.

There are four basic chords for each of the fifteen (15) Major Scales. They are created in the following ways.

Major Chords

Major chords are composed of the 1st, Major 3rd, and Perfect 5th notes of the Major Scale played simultaneously.

Ex. #1:

C Major

1 2 3 4 5 6 7 8   Root position   1st inversion   2nd inversion
                   1st in bass   3rd in bass   5th in bass

Minor Chords

Minor chords are composed of the 1st, Minor 3rd (½ step lower), and Perfect 5th notes of the Major Scale.

Ex. #2:

Cm (m = minor)

1 2 m3 4 5 6 7 8   Root   1st inversion   2nd inversion

Diminished Chords

Diminished chords are composed of the 1st, Minor 3rd, and Diminished 5th (½ step lower) of the Major Scale.

Ex. #3:

Co (o = diminished)

1   m3   d5   Root   1st inversion   2nd inversion

Augmented Chords

The Augmented chord is composed of the 1st, Major 3rd, and Augmented 5th (½ step higher) of the Major Scale.

Ex. #4:

C+ (+ = augmented)

1   3   5   Root   1st inversion   2nd inversion

For more information on Chord Construction - See Pg. 80.

MINOR SCALES

For every Major Scale there will be three Relative Minor Scales.

The Relative Minor Scale will start on the 6th tone of the Major Scale. It will also have the same key signature.

C Major

A minor (Natural)

Same as Natural Minor except raise the 7th note ½ step ascending and descending the scale.

A minor (Harmonic)

Same as Natural Minor except raise the 6th and 7th notes ascending the scale and natural descending the scale.

A minor (Melodic)

G Major *

D Major

E minor (Natural)

B minor (Natural)

E minor (Harmonic)

B minor (Harmonic)

E minor (Melodic)

B minor (Melodic)

*Sharps (♯) are shown next to notes as a reminder for the beginner to play these notes sharp (♯) as indicated in the key signature.

A Major

E Major

F♯ minor (Natural)

C♯ minor (Natural)

F♯ minor (Harmonic)

C♯ minor (Harmonic)

F♯ minor (Melodic)

C♯ minor (Melodic)

B Major

F♯ Major

G♯ minor (Natural)

D♯ minor (Natural)

G♯ minor (Harmonic)

D♯ minor (Harmonic)

G♯ minor (Melodic)

D♯ minor (Melodic)

68

C# Major

F Major

A# minor (Natural)

D minor (Natural)

A# minor (Harmonic)

D minor (Harmonic)

A# minor (Melodic)

D minor (Melodic)

* **Bb Major**

Eb Major

G minor (Natural)

C minor (Natural)

G minor (Harmonic)

C minor (Harmonic)

G minor (Melodic)

C minor (Melodic)

*Remember to play all notes flat (♭) as indicated in key signature.

Ab Major

Db Major

F minor (Natural)

Bb minor (Natural)

F minor (Harmonic)

Bb minor (Harmonic)

F minor (Melodic)

Bb minor (Melodic)

Gb Major

Cb Major

Eb minor (Natural)

Ab minor (Natural)

Eb minor (Harmonic)

Ab minor (Harmonic)

Eb minor (Melodic)

Ab minor (Melodic)

MINOR KEYS

The minor Keys will be based on the minor scales discussed earlier. Because of the construction of these scales, various chords will be created.

Ex. #1:

Key of A minor

The chords generally used in popular music are the ones in the Harmonic minor.

B minor (Harmonic)

I	II	III	IV	V	VI	VII
Bm	C#o	D+	Em	F#	G	A#o

F# minor (Harmonic)

I	II	III	IV	V	VI	VII
F#m	G#o	A+	Bm	C#	D	E#o

C# minor (Harmonic)

I	II	III	IV	V	VI	VII
C#m	D#o	E+	F#m	G#	A	B#o

G# minor (Harmonic)

I	II	III	IV	V	VI	VII
G#m	A#o	B+	C#m	D#	E	F×o

D# minor (Harmonic)

I	II	III	IV	V	VI	VII
D#m	E#o	F#+	G#m	A#	B	C×o

A# minor (Harmonic)

I	II	III	IV	V	VI	VII
A#m	B#o	C#+	D#m	E#	F#	G×o

D minor (Harmonic)

I	II	III	IV	V	VI	VII
Dm	Eo	F+	Gm	A	Bb	C#o

G minor (Harmonic)

I	II	III	IV	V	VI	VII
Gm	Ao	Bb+	Cm	D	Eb	F#o

C minor (Harmonic)

I	II	III	IV	V	VI	VII
Cm	Do	Eb+	Fm	G	Ab	Bo

F minor (Harmonic)

I	II	III	IV	V	VI	VII
Fm	Go	Ab+	Bbm	C	Db	Eo

Bb minor (Harmonic)

I	II	III	IV	V	VI	VII
Bbm	Co	Db+	Ebm	F	Gb	Ao

Eb minor (Harmonic)

I	II	III	IV	V	VI	VII
Ebm	Fo	Gb+	Abm	Bb	Cb	Do

Ab minor (Harmonic)

I	II	III	IV	V	VI	VII
Abm	Bbo	Cb+	Dbm	Eb	Fb	Go

The Following Chord Chart Lists The Major Keys and the Chords in Them.

Key	I	IIm	IIIm	IV	V	VIm	VII°
C	C	Dm	Em	F	G	Am	B°
G	G	Am	Bm	C	D	Em	F#°
D	D	Em	F#m	G	A	Bm	C#°
A	A	Bm	C#m	D	E	F#m	G#°
E	E	F#m	G#m	A	B	C#m	D#°
B	B	C#m	D#m	E	F#	G#m	A#°
F#	F#	G#m	A#m	B	C#	D#m	E#°
C#	C#	D#m	E#m	F#	G#	A#m	B#°
F	F	Gm	Am	Bb	C	Dm	E°
Bb	Bb	Cm	Dm	Eb	F	Gm	A°
Eb	Eb	Fm	Gm	Ab	Bb	Cm	D°
Ab	Ab	Bbm	C	Db	Eb	Fm	G°
Db	Db	Ebm	Fm	Gb	Ab	Bbm	C°
Gb	Gb	Abm	Bbm	Cb	Db	Ebm	F°
Cb	Cb	Dbm	Ebm	Fb	Gb	Abm	Bb°

The Following Chord Chart Lists the Chords in the Minor Keys (Harmonic).

Key	Im	II°	III+	IVm	V	VI	VII°
Am	Am	B°	C+	Dm	E	F	G#°
Em	Em	F#°	G+	Am	B	C	D#°
Bm	Bm	C#°	D+	Em	F#	G	A#°
F#m	F#m	G#°	A+	Bm	C#	D	E#°
C#m	C#m	D#°	E+	F#m	G#	A	B#°
D#m	D#m	E#°	F#+	G#m	A#	B	C#°
A#m	A#m	B#°	C#+	D#m	E#	F#	G#°
Dm	Dm	E°	F+	Gm	A	Bb	C#°
Gm	Gm	A°	Bb+	Cm	D	Eb	F#°
Cm	Cm	D°	Eb+	Fm	G	Ab	B°
Fm	Fm	G°	Ab+	Bbm	C	Db	E°
Bbm	Bbm	C°	Db+	Ebm	F	Gb	A°
Ebm	Ebm	F°	Gb+	Abm	Bb	Cb	D°
Abm	Abm	Bb°	Cb+	Dbm	Eb	Fb	G°

MODES

In search of **new** and **interesting material**, modern **composers use scales** and **keys** <u>other</u> <u>than</u> the **commonly used Major and Minor**. Among this new material, **the modes** and **their keys** are **very popular**. They were **first used in ancient Greece** and then **later on in medieval times**. A **new interest** was **revived in them** mainly **through their use** in the **music of Debussey** and the **other composers** in the **Impressionistic Style**.

EXAMPLE ON "C"   **MODES GENERATED BY MAJOR SCALE**

IONIAN- MAJOR

"DORIAN" - START ON 2nd TONE OF
MAJOR - EX. D DORIAN

"PHRYGIAN" - START ON 3rd TONE OF
MAJOR SCALE - EX. E PHRYGIAN

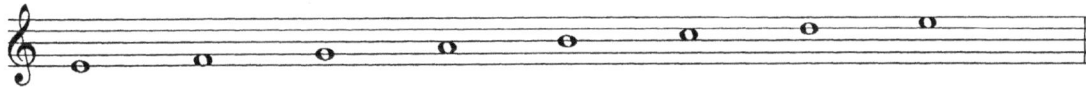

"LYDIAN" - START ON 4th TONE OF
MAJOR SCALE - EX. F LYDIAN

"MIXOLYDIAN" - START ON 5th TONE OF
MAJOR SCALE - EX. G MIXOLYDIAN

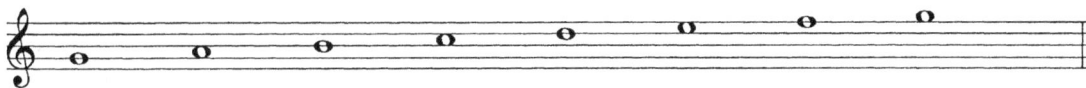

"AEOLIAN" (NATURAL MINOR)
SEE PG. 66

"LOCRIAN" - START ON 7th TONE
OF MAJOR SCALE - EX. B LOCRIAN

MODAL KEYS

Keys are **created from** the **modes** in the **same way major** and **minor keys** are **formed**. Since the **major and minor keys** are **discussed** on **Pg.** 63. **and** the **Locrian**, with its **diminished** I **chord not practical**, we will now **look at** the **four modes** that are the **most commonly used**.

"DORIAN"

The **Dorian Mode** (2nd to 9th note of a major scale - natural minor with a raised 6th) is **distinguished** because of **its 6th step**. For a **melody to sound Dorian**, this **characteristic** should be **emphasized**.

DORIAN SCALE ON "D"

KEY OF "D" DORIAN

I	II	III	IV	V	VI	VII
Dm	Em	F	F	Am	B°	C

PRIMARY CHORDS	I - II - IV
SECONDARY CHORDS	III - Vm - VII
DIMINISHED	VI°

"PHRYGIAN"

The **Phrygian Mode** (3rd to 10th note of a major scale - natural minor with a lowered 2nd) is **distinguished** because of **its second step**. For a **melody to sound Phrygian**, this **characteristic** should be **emphasized.**

PHRYGIAN SCALE ON "E"

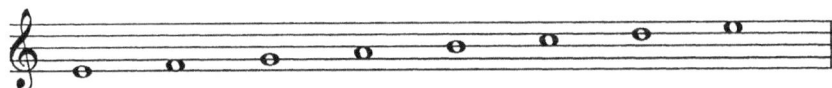

KEY OF E PHRYGIAN

I	II	III	IV	V	VI	VII
Em	F	G	Am	B°	C	Dm

PRIMARY CHORDS	I - II - VIIm
SECONDARY CHORDS	III - IVm - VI
DIMINISHED	V°

"LYDIAN"

The **Lydian Mode** (4th to 11th note of a major scale - major scale with a raised 4th) is **distinguished** because of **its fourth step**. For a **melody to sound Lydian**, this **characteristic** should be **emphasized**.

LYDIAN SCALE ON "F"

KEY OF F LYDIAN

I	II	III	IV	V	VI	VII
F	G	Am	B°	C	Dm	Em

PRIMARY CHORDS	I – II – VIIm
SECONDARY CHORDS	IIIm – V – VIm
DIMINISHED	IV°

"MIXOLYDIAN"

The **Mixolydian mode** (5th to 12th note of a major scale - a major scale with a lowered 7th) is **distinguished** because of **its 7th step**. For a **melody to sound Mixolydian**, this **characteristic** should be **emphasized**.

MIXOLYDIAN SCALE ON "G"

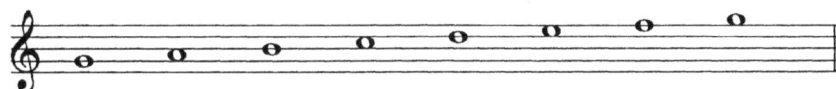

KEY OF "G" MIXOLYDIAN

I	II	III	IV	V	VI	VII
G	Am	B°	C	Dm	Em	F

PRIMARY CHORDS   I - Vm - VII

SECONDARY CHORDS   IIm - IV - VIm

DIMINISHED   III°

ADDITIONAL SCALE MATERIAL (SYNTHETIC)

The **following scales**, which have come into **use in varying styles of music**, can be **useful** in **certain situations**. All **scales** are shown **starting on C**; however, **they can start on any note**, the **same as** the **major and minor scales**. They **can** also **create** their own keys by simply **building chords upon each note**. To **transpose** *any* scale, just **start on the note you select**, and ascend the **scale, keeping the same interval makeup** as shown. **Each scale** will **generate** its **own set of modes** in the **same manner as** we have seen with the **major scales**.

HUNGARIAN MAJOR

A2   m2   M2   m2   M2   m2   M2

EIGHT-TONE SPANISH

m2   M2   m2   m2   m2   M2   M2   M2

SYMETRICAL

m2   M2   m2   M2   m2   M2   m2   M2

PENTATONIC

M2   M2   m3   M2   m3

PELOG

m2   M2   M3   m2   M3

HIRAJOSHI

M2   m2   M3   m2   M3

KUMOI

M2   m2   M3   M2   m3

NEAPOLITAN MAJOR

m2   M2   M2   M2   M2   M2   m2

NEAPOLITAN MINOR

m2   M2   M2   M2   m2   A2   m2

ORIENTAL

m2   A2   m2   m2   A2   m2   M2

DOUBLE HARMONIC

m2   A2   m2   M2   m2   A2   m2

ENIGMATIC

m2   A2   M2   M2   M2   m2   m2

HUNGARIAN MINOR

M2   m2   A2   m2   m2   A2   m2

MAJOR LOCRIAN

M2   M2   m2   m2   M2   M2   M2

LYDIAN MINOR

M2   M2   M2   m2   m2   M2   M2

OVERTONE

M2   M2   M2   m2   M2   m2   M2

LEADING WHOLE-TONE

M2   M2   M2   M2   M2   M2

CHORD EXTENSIONS

We will exchange the most commonly used substitutions in contemporary music for the basic chords. Composers freely substitute chords with higher forms of the original. This creates new and interesting tonal colors.

Ex. #1: C major could become C6 – Cmaj7 – Cmaj9 – Cmaj13 – Cma7-5

The following list shows the most common chord substitutions. Your own taste and ear will be the governing factor when selecting chords. The notes of your melody should reflect these higher chord tones when the chord is played.

I	IIm	IIIm	IV	V	VIm	VII°
I6	IIm7	IIIm7	IV6	V7	VIm7	VII°7
Imaj7	IIm9		IVmaj7	V7-5	VIm9	VII$^\emptyset$7
Imaj9	IIm7-5		IVmaj9	V7+5		
Imaj13			IVmaj13	V9		
Imaj7-5				V9-5		
Imaj/9				V9+5		
I6/9				V7-9		
				V7$^{-9}_{-5}$		
				V7$^{-9}_{+5}$		
				V7sus4		
				V11		
				V13		
				V13-9		

www.ingramcontent.com/pod-product-compliance
Lightning Source LLC
Chambersburg PA
CBHW081137090426
42742CB00015BA/2870